THE BEST OF WORLD SOCCER

THE BEST MANAGERS OF WORLD SOCCER

BY PATRICK DONNELLY

SportsZone
An Imprint of Abdo Publishing
abdobooks.com

abdobooks.com

Published by Abdo Publishing, a division of ABDO, PO Box 398166, Minneapolis, Minnesota 55439.

Printed in the United States of America, North Mankato, Minnesota.
102023
012024

THIS BOOK CONTAINS RECYCLED MATERIALS

Cover Photo: Tom Jenkins/Getty Images Sport/Getty Images
Interior Photos: James Williamson/AMA/Getty Images Sport/Getty Images, 4–5; W. E. Turton/Topical Press Agency/Hulton Archive/Getty Images, 6; Fox Photos/Hulton Archive/Getty Images, 8; Hulton Archive/Getty Images, 9; English Heritage/Heritage Images/Hulton Archive/Getty Images, 10; Alex Livesey/Getty Images Sport/Getty Images, 12; Gianni Ferrari/Cover/Getty Images, 13; VI-Images/Getty Images Sport/Getty Images, 14; Duncan Raban/Allsport/Hulton Archive/Getty Images, 16–17; sampics/Corbis Sport/Getty Images, 18; Claudio Villa/Getty Images Sport/Getty Images, 20; Alessandro Sabattini/Getty Images Sport/Getty Images, 21; Bernard Bisson/Sygma/Getty Images, 23; David Cannon/Allsport/David Cannon Collection/Getty Images, 24–25; Shaun Botterill/Allsport/Getty Images Sport/Getty Images, 26; Shaun Botterill/Getty Images Sport/Getty Images, 29, 30; Michael Regan/Getty Images Sport/Getty Images, 32; Isaac Parkin/Manchester City FC/Getty Images, 34; Marvin Ibo Guengoer/GES Sportfoto/Getty Images Sport/Getty Images, 35; Andy Mead/ISI Photos/Getty Images Sport/Getty Images, 36–37; Rick Stewart/Allsport/Getty Images Sport/Getty Images, 38; Danny Gohlke/Bongarts/Getty Images, 40; Doug Pensinger/Getty Images Sport/Getty Images, 42; Filipe Farinha Getty Images Sport/Getty Images, 43; Maja Hitij/Getty Images Sport/Getty Images, 45

Editor: Luke Hanlon
Series Designers: Karli Kruse and Joshua Olson

Library of Congress Control Number: 2023939434

Publisher's Cataloging-in-Publication Data

Names: Donnelly, Patrick, author.
Title: The best managers of world soccer / by Patrick Donnelly
Description: Minneapolis, Minnesota: Abdo Publishing, 2024 | Series: The best of world soccer | Includes online resources and index.
Identifiers: ISBN 9781098292256 (lib. bdg.) | ISBN 9798384910190 (ebook)
Subjects: LCSH: Soccer--Juvenile literature. | Professional sports--Juvenile literature. | Soccer managers--Juvenile literature. | Soccer--Coaches--Juvenile literature. | Soccer--Records--Juvenile literature.
Classification: DDC 796.334--dc23

TABLE OF CONTENTS

CHAPTER 1

PIONEERS 4

CHAPTER 2

THE NEW BREED 16

CHAPTER 3

MODERN MEN'S MANAGERS .. 24

CHAPTER 4

TRAILBLAZING WOMEN'S MANAGERS 36

GLOSSARY 46

MORE INFORMATION 47

ONLINE RESOURCES 47

INDEX 48

ABOUT THE AUTHOR 48

CHAPTER 1

PIONEERS

Managing a soccer team is a difficult job at the highest levels. Club managers have to game-plan each week for new opponents, stay up with the current trends in tactics, and help the sporting director identify which players to sign. The manager then needs to mold those players, who might

Managers can experience a lot of stress during games.

come from all over the globe, into a winning team. Meanwhile, national team managers get very little time to work with players. They also have a limited pool of players to pick from, since the players all have to be from that country. Often national teams get to practice only a few weeks per year. But when big tournaments such as the World Cup or Women's World Cup roll around, all eyes are on them.

Because of that pressure, many managers don't last long. But those who are successful can stay with a club or national team for many years. And some of them gain truly legendary status in the sport.

THE GREAT INNOVATOR

Soccer as we know it today started in the mid-1800s in England. Though some women played in the early days, for a long time the sport was mostly limited to men. And by the early 1900s, athletic clubs began forming men's soccer teams to represent them. Usually members of the club recruited players they wanted on their side. Managers didn't have much say in player selection.

Thanks to managers such as Herbert Chapman, that began to change. Chapman managed four teams in England from 1907 to 1934. He was one of the first managers to focus on the

Herbert Chapman, *far left*, poses for a team photo with Huddersfield Town in 1922.

importance of physical fitness in his players. He was also a big supporter of a competition among European teams. At the time, teams mostly played opponents from nearby cities. Even the tradition of opposing teams walking onto the field side by side was Chapman's idea.

Chapman also had a great impact on the field. In soccer's early days, the game was relatively disorganized. Few teams used set lineups like those seen today. Chapman knew that his players would be more successful if they had more structure on the field. He invented what became known as the "W-M" formation. In the W-M, the five attacking players form a W shape, with three forwards at the top and two midfielders behind them. The defenders form an M shape, with three players on the back line and two midfielders in front of them. The formation has changed and grown in the decades since. However, one popular formation used today, known as the 3–4–3, is similar to Chapman's original idea.

Chapman won two English First Division titles with Huddersfield Town in the 1920s. He then won two more in the early 1930s with Arsenal. He might have won more, but Chapman died suddenly in January 1934. The Arsenal team he built won three more titles in the 1930s, including the year he passed away.

THE METHOD

Italian Vittorio Pozzo put his own stamp on the sport in the 1930s. Pozzo managed top club teams such as AC Milan and Torino, but he was best known for his time leading Italy's men's national team. Pozzo fell in love with the game while studying in England. And some of the tactics he used were similar to the English game. Pozzo became famous for the *Metodo*, or "Method" alignment. It was similar to Chapman's

W-M formation. However, it featured three halfbacks and two fullbacks, creating more of a "W-W."

Pozzo used the *Metodo* to lead Italy to the World Cup title in 1934. That strategy worked again in 1938 as Italy defended its crown. That made Pozzo the first manager to lead a team to back-to-back World Cup championships. In between the two World Cups, he also guided Italy to victory at the 1936 Olympics in Berlin, Germany.

Vittorio Pozzo, *far left*, talks to his Italy players before extra time of the 1934 World Cup final began. Italy went on to beat Czechoslovakia 2–1.

BUSBY, BILL, AND BOB

Matt Busby poses with the European Cup trophy in 1968.

Long before Manchester United became one of the most recognizable clubs in the world, Matt Busby built the team into a powerhouse, not once but twice. Busby took over a struggling Manchester United in 1945. Over the next decade, the Scotsman showed a knack for developing young players. By the end of the 1956–57 season, his teams had won three English First Division titles. Even better, most of his best players were in their early 20s. The press dubbed the team the "Busby Babes," and it looked set to be a force for years to come.

Heading home from a match in what is now Serbia in February 1958, the team's plane crashed in Munich, Germany. Of the 44 people on board, 23 were killed, including eight Manchester United players. Two others suffered career-ending injuries. After spending two months in a hospital, Busby returned to build the team once again.

Seven years after the crash, he fielded another championship team in 1964–65. United, led by new stars George Best, crash survivor Bobby Charlton, and Denis Law, won the league title again two seasons later. That core added

A statue of Matt Busby has been outside Manchester United's stadium since 1996.

GEORGE RAMSAY

The first man ever hired and paid to manage a soccer club was George Ramsay. The Scotsman was captain of Aston Villa in Birmingham, England, but an injury forced him to retire. In 1886 the club hired him to lead its transition from amateur to professional soccer. Ramsay managed Aston Villa for the next 41 years, winning six league titles.

a championship in the European Cup, which is now known as the Champions League, in 1968. Busby finally left Manchester United in 1971. His time at United set the standard that the club built on in years to come.

Not far from Manchester, Liverpool also became a powerhouse in the 1960s. And it had not one but two great managers to thank for it. When Bill Shankly took over in 1959, Liverpool was in England's Second Division. Shankly turned things around by changing the culture of the club. The Scotsman made sure fans at the stadium felt like they were included. He encouraged the fans to motivate the team with cheers. To this day, the "Kop" end of Liverpool's home stadium,

On September 1, 2013, the Kop end at Anfield honors the 100th anniversary of Bill Shankly's birth by recreating the pose of Shankly's statue outside the stadium.

Anfield, is considered one of the most enthusiastic cheering sections in the world.

Shankly retired in 1974 after winning three league titles. He also led his team to two championships in the Football Association (FA) Cup, a tournament featuring teams from all levels of English soccer.

For all of Shankly's success, his assistant manager Bob Paisley took over and made Liverpool even more successful. While Shankly was the master motivator, Paisley thrived by outsmarting opponents with his tactics and game planning.

By the time he retired in 1983, Paisley had won six league titles and three European Cups.

GAME CHANGERS

England wasn't the only place where managers were establishing powerful club identities. Argentine Helenio Herrera managed 12 different clubs in his career. But he is best known as the manager of Italian team Inter Milan in the 1960s and 1970s. Like Shankly, Herrera wanted to make the fans feel they were part of the experience. He urged them to come to matches and cheer passionately, calling them the "12th man." He also perfected an Italian playing style known as *Catenaccio*. Playing this way, his teams defended with five players then launched quick counterattacks to score goals. Many managers still use this strategy. With it Herrera and Inter Milan dominated Serie A, the top league in Italy, in the 1960s. Inter won the league title

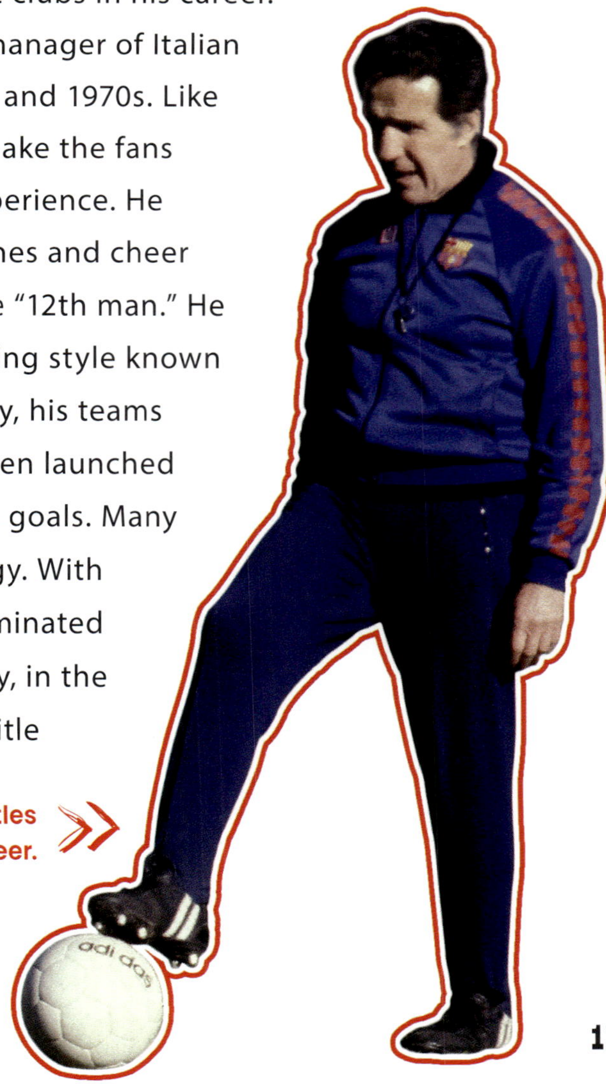

Helenio Herrera won seven league titles in his managerial career.

Rinus Michels walks with the European Championship trophy after leading the Netherlands to victory in 1988.

three times from 1963 to 1966. His defensive style also led Inter to consecutive European Cups in 1964 and 1965.

However, no manager changed soccer tactics more than Rinus Michels of the Netherlands. Before Michels's managerial career, most soccer teams played with strict positions. Defenders rarely joined the attack, and forwards didn't come back to defend.

First with Amsterdam-based club Ajax in the Netherlands and then with the Netherlands men's national team, Michels put together a new system. His players ran all over the field. They covered spaces left open by teammates who had moved into new areas. The strategy came to be known as "Total Football."

Michels led Ajax to three straight European Cups from 1971 to 1973 playing that way. The Netherlands nearly won the 1974 World Cup with Michels coaching. He left the national team after finishing as runner-up to West Germany. But Michels returned in the 1980s and had more success with his home country. Michels led the Netherlands to the final of the 1988 European Championship. Fittingly, a defender and an attacker scored to lift the Netherlands to a 2–0 victory against the Soviet Union. That was the first major trophy in the country's history. By the time he retired for good in 1992, Michels's influence on the sport was felt all over the globe.

CHAPTER 2

THE NEW BREED

Many great club managers have taken over teams in lower divisions and brought them to the top. Englishman Brian Clough did it with two different teams. Along the way, he made sure to tell everyone who would listen just how great of a manager he was.

Brian Clough, *right*, and his assistant manager, Peter Taylor, won seven trophies when they worked together at Nottingham Forest.

Derby County hired Clough to be the team's manager in 1967. Derby hadn't had much success in England's First Division. But Clough's assistant, Peter Taylor, had a gift for identifying talented players. And Clough was a strategic genius who knew how to use them. Together Clough and Taylor not only reached England's top level but won it in 1971–72. It was Derby's first championship. A year later, Clough's underdog club, nicknamed the Rams, reached the European Cup semifinals.

Clough was perhaps one of the most confident managers ever. He once told an interviewer, "I wouldn't say I'm the best manager in the world, but I'm in the top one." But his attitude sometimes bothered his employers. Clough angrily left Derby in 1973. He then crashed out of two clubs in two years. In that time, he won only 13 of 38 games.

Clough and Taylor ended up at Nottingham Forest in 1975. Four years later, the duo had led it from the Second Division to champion of Europe. Forest repeated as European Cup champion in 1980.

TROPHY CASES

Udo Lattek was well on his way to a successful teaching career in the early 1960s. Then he decided to take a break and try

Bayern Munich fans honor Udo Lattek days after he died in 2015.

coaching soccer. Within a few years, he was an assistant for the West Germany team that finished as runner-up at the 1966 World Cup. Along the way, he made friends with several of the team's best players, such as defender Franz Beckenbauer.

Four years later, Bayern Munich needed a new coach. Beckenbauer suggested that Lattek get the job. At the time, not many people knew who Lattek was. But Bayern hired him. Now he was in charge of West Germany's best club. Even after

Lattek won a European Cup and three titles in the Bundesliga, the top German league, from 1972 to 1974, many fans gave credit to the team's players, not Lattek.

When Bayern struggled the next season, Lattek was fired. Critics called him a fraud. Lattek proved them wrong by taking over one of Bayern's rivals, Borussia Mönchengladbach. With his new club, Lattek won back-to-back league titles in 1975–76 and 1976–77. In 1979 the team won Europe's second-best club competition, the UEFA Cup. Today that tournament is known as the Europa League.

At that time, there were three major European competitions for clubs. Lattek won the third in 1982 as manager of Barcelona in Spain. His victory in the Cup Winners' Cup made him the first manager to have won all three competitions.

DOUBLE CHAMPIONS

Three men have won the World Cup as a player and a manager. Mário Zagallo of Brazil was the first. He won as a player in 1958 and 1962 and then managed Brazil to a title in 1970. Franz Beckenbauer captained the West German champions of 1974. He then won the 1990 World Cup as West Germany's manager. France's Didier Deschamps won the World Cup as a player in 1998 and as a manager 20 years later.

Bayern Munich brought Lattek back in the mid-1980s. He won three more Bundesliga titles with the famous club before retiring in 1987 with 14 major championships. He had long since proved he belonged.

Just three years after Lattek became the first man to win all three major European competitions, Italian Giovanni Trapattoni became the second. His Juventus teams had already won the UEFA Cup in 1977 and the Cup Winners' Cup in 1984. In 1985 "Il Trap" led Juventus to victory in the European Cup.

Trapattoni was known for a very defensive style of play. He was also known for his superstitions. He managed Italy at the 2002 World Cup. Trapattoni brought a bottle of holy water onto the field for every match. The bottle was given to him by his sister, who was a nun. It didn't

During Giovanni Trapattoni's long career, he managed club teams in Italy, Germany, and Portugal.

work, as Italy lost in the round of 16. But that was a rare failure for the Italian, who won league titles in four countries during his nearly 40-year career.

TACTICAL GENIUSES

While Juventus was thriving under Trapattoni, another traditional Italian power was struggling. In 1987 AC Milan hired Arrigo Sacchi to turn things around. The Italian media wasn't

AC Milan players lift Arrigo Sacchi in the air after they won the Serie A title in 1988.

convinced. Sacchi had never been a player. He'd actually spent most of his life selling shoes. The 41-year-old coach shook off his doubters, saying, "I never realized that to be a jockey, you had to be a horse first."

Most Italian managers favored defensive soccer. Sacchi was different. He told his players to pressure their opponents high up the field and play a fast, attacking game. AC Milan won the Serie A title in his first season. The team followed that up by winning the European Cup in 1989 and 1990. The next year Sacchi was hired by the Italian men's national team. He took it to the final of the 1994 World Cup before losing to Brazil. Along the way, Sacchi's attacking style influenced many managers of the next generation.

Johan Cruyff's abilities as a player were legendary. The Dutch forward was the star of Rinus Michels's "Total Football" system for both Ajax and the Netherlands national team in the 1960s and 1970s. Many consider him one of the sport's all-time greats.

After Cruyff retired, he moved quickly into coaching. He started at Ajax and won two Dutch Cups in the mid-1980s. He then took his system to Barcelona, another one of his former clubs, in 1989.

At the time, Barcelona was a struggling team. Cruyff quickly changed things. Playing his fluid attacking system, the

Cruyff managed Barcelona for nine seasons from 1988 to 1996.

team won La Liga, Spain's top league, four times in a row in the early 1990s. But Cruyff also made sure Barcelona's youth players were trained just like the first-team players. That way when they reached the top level, they already knew the team's strategy. Soon Barcelona's academy, known as *La Masia,* "the Farmhouse," became one of the best in the world. It would eventually turn out such great players as Andrés Iniesta, Sergio Busquets, Lionel Messi, and Xavi.

CHAPTER 3

MODERN MEN'S MANAGERS

After Matt Busby left Manchester United in the 1970s, the team struggled. The club even spent a season in the Second Division. By 1986 the Red Devils still hadn't won another First Division title. To try to change that, the club hired another Scottish manager, Alex Ferguson. After the team

Alex Ferguson's 13 first-division league titles are the most by any manager in the history of English soccer.

struggled for a few more years, fans wanted Ferguson fired. But the club stuck with him. By 1992–93 he had a group of young stars ready to challenge for titles.

They would do that in a "new" league. That year the teams in England's top division broke away from the rest of the English Football League system and created the Premier League. Over time it has become the most popular league in the world.

Ferguson's United teams were a huge reason why. His squad won the league in eight of its first 11 seasons. And in 1999, Manchester United won the Premier League, FA Cup, and Champions League in the same year. No English team had ever achieved that accomplishment, which was nicknamed the "treble." He received a knighthood from Queen Elizabeth II shortly after winning the treble. After that, he was known as Sir Alex Ferguson.

Ferguson was a skilled tactical manager, but he was also known as a master motivator. That sometimes involved losing his temper. His famous halftime rants became known as "hair dryer" moments because his screaming was said to blow players' hair back. But he knew how to motivate in other ways. Once before a match against Tottenham Hotspur, Ferguson's pep talk was just three words. Knowing his team had usually

Ferguson holds the trophies for the FA Cup and the Premier League in 1999.

dominated Spurs, Ferguson said calmly, “Lads, it’s Tottenham.” United won the match.

In the modern era, many managers, even successful ones, don’t stay at a club for very long. Ferguson spent 27 years at Manchester United. In that time, his teams won 13 Premier League titles, five FA Cups, and two Champions League crowns.

OTTMAR HITZFELD

As Bayern Munich manager, Ottmar Hitzfeld lost the 1999 Champions League final. But Hitzfeld didn't lose much else. He won two Bundesliga titles and a Champions League with German club Borussia Dortmund in the mid-1990s. Hitzfeld also won five Bundesliga championships and the 2001 Champions League with Bayern Munich.

When one of his former players, Gary Neville, was asked to name Ferguson's best accomplishments, he said it was impossible. "As soon as you decide on one, you come up with another that surpasses it," Neville said.

A GLOBAL FLAIR

For many years, club soccer in England was known for being very British. It was difficult for foreign players to break through. Foreign managers had an even tougher time. Arsène Wenger helped change that.

Few had heard of the Frenchman when London club Arsenal hired him in 1996. A newspaper headline in London read

"Arsène Who?" After all, he had most recently been managing in Japan. Wenger quickly established himself, however. His emphasis on nutrition and fitness was new to many in English soccer. He also turned Arsenal into one of the first truly international teams in England. Over the years he signed players from 26 countries. What fans remember most fondly, however, was Arsenal's attacking flair under Wenger.

Wenger coached at Arsenal until 2018, winning three Premier League titles. His 2003–04 championship squad finished the season with 26 wins, 12 draws, and zero losses. That Arsenal team, which became known as "The Invincibles," was the first in England to finish a season undefeated since 1888–89.

Wenger's ideas influenced many managers who followed him. He also helped open the door for other international managers to join the Premier League. One of the most successful of those managers was José Mourinho. The Portuguese manager made his name by guiding one of his country's top clubs, FC Porto, to an unlikely Champions League win in 2004. The next season, Chelsea hired him to turn the London club into an English powerhouse.

English fans bristled at Mourinho's blunt and outspoken style. He didn't win over the media when he called himself the "Special One" in his first press conference at Chelsea. However,

Arsène Wenger, *left*, and José Mourinho often clashed when their two London-based clubs played each other.

Mourinho lived up to his own hype. The manager used his favored defensive style, followed by quick counterattacks, to guide Chelsea to Premier League titles in his first two seasons. The Blues won the FA Cup in his third. Even after his abrasive personality got him fired early in the 2007–08 season, Mourinho was still seen as a top coach. Italian power Inter Milan hired him in 2008–09. In his second season he led the club to a historic treble—victory in Serie A, the Coppa Italia,

Mourinho, *left*, jumps in celebration after Inter Milan won the Champions League in 2010.

and the Champions League. He went on to coach at several other big clubs after that, including Manchester United, Real Madrid, and Chelsea again.

ITALIAN GIANTS

In the 1990s and 2000s, two Italian coaches seemed to win everywhere they went. Fabio Capello was known as a stern coach who wasn't particularly friendly with his players. But his methods were successful. Capello started his career in his home country. There he won four straight Serie A titles and a Champions League with AC Milan in the 1990s. He then moved to Real Madrid and won a league title in Spain. After leaving Real Madrid, he moved back to Italy and won another Serie A title with Roma. Though he added two more with Juventus, those were later stripped as part of a widespread cheating scandal. Nonetheless, by the time he went back to Real Madrid and won another league title in 2007, Capello's legacy was cemented as one of the all-time greats.

MARCELO BIELSA

Marcelo Bielsa's intense, aggressive coaching style isn't for everybody. Sometimes it works spectacularly. Other times it flames out. Either way, the manager refuses to change. The Argentine is unapologetically stubborn. His successes, often coaching lower-profile teams, has led to fierce devotion from players, fans, and other managers.

Carlo Ancelotti often kept a calm demeanor on the sidelines regardless of how his team was performing.

However, Capello doesn't think he is Italy's all-time best coach. When asked, he gave that honor to Carlo Ancelotti. "Don Carlo" began managing in 1995 and has gone on to coach many of the biggest teams in Europe. He has had spells with Juventus, AC Milan, Real Madrid, Chelsea, Paris Saint-Germain, and Bayern Munich, among others. While his stretches with each club were often short, they were usually successful. Ancelotti has won top-level league championships in every country in which he's managed. And he was the first manager to win the Champions League four times.

PEP'S WORLD

Pep Guardiola developed as a player at Barcelona's famous La Masia academy. Under the club's influential coach, Johan Cruyff, Guardiola became a standout midfielder for the senior team. Later Guardiola became a manager himself. He used Cruyff's same philosophies of possession, quick passing, and constant movement. This style became known as "tiki-taka."

Guardiola got his start as a manager with Barcelona's reserve team. After one season in charge, he was promoted to the senior team manager in 2008. His tactics made star forward Lionel Messi even better. Barcelona became a European powerhouse under Guardiola. He lifted Barcelona to Champions League titles in 2009 and 2011. In 2013 he moved to Germany's most successful team, Bayern Munich. Over his three seasons there, the team won three league titles. Then Guardiola took over English club Manchester City in 2016.

Manchester City had long been a mediocre club. But new owners had taken over in 2008 with big aspirations—and a big checkbook. They hired Guardiola to fulfill those goals. Under the new manager, City became England's strongest team. The 2017–18 squad became the first in Premier League history to earn 100 points in the standings. The one knock on Guardiola was that he had never won a European title without Messi, considered by many to be the world's best player. Finally, in

Unlike Ancelotti, Pep Guardiola is often dramatic on the sideline during matches.

Guardiola kisses the Champions League trophy after leading Manchester City to the championship in 2023.

2023, that changed. Guardiola led City to championships in the Premier League, FA Cup, and Champions League. That put City in an exclusive club with Manchester United as the only English teams to win the treble. Having also led Barcelona to a treble in 2009, that also made Guardiola the only manager to achieve that feat twice.

CHAPTER 4

TRAILBLAZING WOMEN'S MANAGERS

Much of soccer's history excludes women. For decades there weren't any professional leagues for women to play in. That was in large part because the game's organizers purposefully kept women out of the game—even in big soccer countries such as Brazil, England, and Germany.

Anson Dorrance coached his 45th season at the University of North Carolina in 2023.

Women finally started getting more opportunities during the 1970s. By the 1980s, the women's game had some real momentum. And so in 1985, the US women's national team was founded. However, that first year didn't go as planned for the Americans. The US team played four games. It tied one and lost three. In an effort to improve, US Soccer turned to Anson Dorrance. As the women's coach at the University of North Carolina, he was in the process of building the college game's most powerful program. The US officials hoped he could do the same with the national team.

A COLLEGE POWER

Anson Dorrance guided the US women to the top of the world. He also kept his University of North Carolina team atop women's college soccer for decades. The Tar Heels won the first women's college national title in 1982. In 2012 they won a record 21st championship. Still under Dorrance, the Tar Heels were national runners-up for the sixth time in 2022.

Tony DiCicco sings "The Star-Spangled Banner" before a US women's national team game in 1995.

Dorrance made his mark on the US team right away. He told his players that they needed to show up to the team's first training camp in top condition or he would cut them. Dorrance needed physically fit players for his intense, high-pressure system. The players responded, and by 1991 the United States was one of the best teams in the world. What is now known as the first Women's World Cup was held in China that year. Dorrance's team pressured its way to victory, outscoring its opponents 25–5.

When the team needed to replace Dorrance in 1994, the job went to his goalkeeping coach, Tony DiCicco. His first major tournament ended in a disappointing semifinal defeat at the 1995 World Cup. He bounced back quickly. The next year's Olympics were the first to include women's soccer. On home soil, DiCicco led the Americans to gold. However, his crowning achievement came in 1999. Back on home soil, this time in the World Cup, DiCicco guided the US women to victory over China in a thrilling penalty shootout final.

PIONEERING WOMEN

The United States' victory over China in 1999 brought on a new, more popular era for women's soccer. However, 14 of the 16 coaches at that year's Women's World Cup were men. One of the few exceptions was Tina Theune-Meyer. Her German team nearly upset the United States in the quarterfinals. Four years later, Theune-Meyer led Germany to its first Women's World Cup title. In doing so, she became the first female coach of a World Cup winner.

That win was part of a string of successes for Theune-Meyer and Germany. They had already won the European Championship in 1997 and 2001. And Theune-Meyer guided the team to another championship in that tournament in 2005.

Germany won two World Cups and five European Championships when either Tina Theune-Meyer, *left*, or Silvia Neid was the team's manager.

Theune-Meyer left her post after that. Assistant Silvia Neid stepped in, and the German team didn't miss a beat. Coaching a team that featured star forward Birgit Prinz and goalkeeper Nadine Angerer, Neid led Germany to a repeat title at the 2007 World Cup. She stayed in the position through 2016, winning two more European Championships along the way before capping her career with a 2016 Olympic gold medal.

MAKING THE SWITCH

Neid was part of a new generation of female coaches who had also been international players. The former midfielder had scored 48 goals in 111 games for Germany. Pia Sundhage was another. She had been a star forward for Sweden during the

EMMA HAYES

Women's club soccer took some time to take off. Now it's thriving in parts of Europe and North America. Emma Hayes took over English team Chelsea in 2012. Under her leadership, the Blues won their first league and Women's FA Cup in 2015. Hayes guided the team to a fifth "double" in 2023.

Pia Sundhage, *middle*, gets emotional during a tribute after she managed her last game for the United States.

1980s and 1990s, scoring 71 goals over 22 years. In 2007 she became manager of the US women's team.

The team was coming off a disappointing performance at that year's World Cup. Sundhage brought an upbeat, positive coaching style. When not practicing, she famously played guitar for her players. She also got results. For years the Americans were known for their physical, attacking style. Sundhage's teams instead worked to maintain possession in the midfield. Under her leadership, the United States won two Olympic gold medals and finished runner-up at the 2011 World Cup. She later managed her native Sweden and then took over as Brazil's coach.

OVER THE HUMP

The manager who beat Sundhage's US team at the 2011 World Cup overcame many obstacles. Norio Sasaki was managing a Japanese team playing for a country that did not have a professional women's league. In addition, Japan had suffered through a terrible earthquake and tsunami a few months prior to the World Cup. Thousands of people had been killed, and the disaster also caused over $200 billion in damage.

After winning the 2011 World Cup, Norio Sasaki guided Japan to the finals at the 2012 Olympics and then the 2015 World Cup.

Few expected Japan to get past two-time defending champion Germany in the quarterfinals. To give his players a sense of who and what they were playing for, Sasaki showed them a slideshow of the destruction. Japan won in extra time. After beating Sweden and the United States, Japan became the first Asian team to win a World Cup. Sasaki became the first Asian manager to win the tournament as well.

Sasaki's Japan team reached the World Cup final again in 2015. By then, Jill Ellis had taken over the US team. Raised in England, Ellis moved to the United States as a teenager in 1981. She began coaching in the late 1980s. After steadily climbing the ranks at the college and US youth national team level, Ellis took over the senior national team job in 2014.

SARINA WIEGMAN

Sarina Wiegman became the first woman to play in 100 games for the Netherlands. As a coach, she led the Netherlands to its first major women's title at the 2017 European Championship. Two years later, her team reached the 2019 World Cup final. Wiegman later took over the England women's team and led it to the 2022 European title and 2023 World Cup final.

Hiring an unproven head coach was a risk. Ellis took her own risks, including changing the team to a more attacking 4–3–3 formation and putting some players in unfamiliar positions. Those moves paid off. The Americans won the 2015 World Cup, giving up just three goals over seven games. The final was a triumphant 5–2 win over Japan.

Jill Ellis won 106 of her 132 games in charge of the US women's national team.

Ellis stayed with the United States through the 2019 World Cup. Only Italy's Vittorio Pozzo had ever won back-to-back World Cups. But after the United States beat the Netherlands 2–0 in the final, Ellis had made history of her own.

Every season presents a chance for a manager to lead their team to glory. Managers also have the opportunity to adapt their strategy and do something the game has never seen before. The ones who can keep up with modern trends and win year after year get remembered as legends.

GLOSSARY

ACADEMY
A program run by a club to train young players and help them improve their skills.

AMATEUR
Something that is done for fun rather than as a job.

CLUB
The team a player competes with outside of his or her national team.

ERA
A period of time in history.

EXTRA TIME
Two 15-minute periods added to a tournament game if the score is tied at the end of regulation.

FEAT
A notable achievement.

FORMATION
The general way a team positions its players on the field.

PROFESSIONAL
Something that is done as a job.

RETIRE
To end one's career.

SHOOTOUT
A series of penalty kicks held after extra time to decide who wins a game.

TACTICAL
Referring to carefully planned actions or strategy.

UNDERDOG
A person or team that is not expected to win.

MORE INFORMATION

BOOKS

Hanlon, Luke. *The Best Men's Players of World Soccer.* Minneapolis, MN: Abdo Publishing, 2024.

Hewson, Anthony K. *GOATs of Soccer.* Minneapolis, MN: Abdo Publishing, 2022.

McDougall, Chrös. *The Best Women's Players of World Soccer.* Minneapolis, MN: Abdo Publishing, 2024.

ONLINE RESOURCES

Booklinks
NONFICTION NETWORK
FREE! ONLINE NONFICTION RESOURCES

To learn more about soccer managers, please visit abdobooklinks.com or scan this QR code. These links are routinely monitored and updated to provide the most current information available.

INDEX

Ancelotti, Carlo, 33
Angerer, Nadine, 41

Beckenbauer, Franz, 18, 19
Best, George, 10
Bielsa, Marcelo, 31
Busby, Matt, 9–11, 24
Busquets, Sergio, 23

Capello, Fabio, 30–31, 33
Chapman, Herbert, 5–7
Charlton, Bobby, 10
Clough, Brian, 16–17
Cruyff, Johan, 22–23, 33

Deschamps, Didier, 19
DiCicco, Tony, 39
Dorrance, Anson, 37, 39

Ellis, Jill, 44–45

Ferguson, Alex, 24–27

Guardiola, Pep, 33–35

Herrera, Helenio, 13, 15
Hitzfeld, Ottmar, 27

Iniesta, Andrés, 23

Lattek, Udo, 17–20
Law, Denis, 10

Messi, Lionel, 23, 33–34
Michels, Rinus, 15, 22
Mourinho, José, 28–30

Neid, Silvia, 41
Neville, Gary, 27

Paisley, Bob, 12–13
Pozzo, Vittorio, 7–8, 45
Prinz, Birgit, 41

Ramsay, George, 11

Sacchi, Arrigo, 21–22
Sasaki, Norio, 43–44
Shankly, Bill, 11–13
Sundhage, Pia, 41–43

Taylor, Peter, 17
Theune-Meyer, Tina, 39–41
Trapattoni, Giovanni, 20–21

Wenger, Arsène, 27–28
Wiegman, Sarina, 44

Xavi, 23

Zagallo, Mário, 19

ABOUT THE AUTHOR

Patrick Donnelly is a freelance writer who lives in Minneapolis, Minnesota.